Original title:
The Glow of Hopeful Skies

Copyright © 2025 Swan Charm
All rights reserved.

Author: Sara Säde
ISBN HARDBACK: 978-9908-1-3004-0
ISBN PAPERBACK: 978-9908-1-3005-7
ISBN EBOOK: 978-9908-1-3006-4

The Promise of a New Awakening

In the dawn's soft glow we rise,
Whispers of hope in azure skies.
Fresh beginnings all around,
In each heartbeat, dreams are found.

Awakening from the night,
Chasing shadows, finding light.
Nature's song begins to swell,
A symphony, all is well.

Life unfurls like petals wide,
With each breath, new worlds collide.
A gentle nudge, a call to stand,
Together we can change this land.

With every step, our paths align,
In unity, our spirits shine.
Embracing futures, bold and bright,
In every heart, ignites the light.

So let us herald this new dawn,
With love and courage, we move on.
In this promise, we believe,
A new awakening, we achieve.

Horizons Bathed in Warmth

Beneath the sun's embrace we bask,
In every shade, a loving task.
Golden rays on fields of green,
Nature's canvas, pure and keen.

The skies above, a tranquil blue,
Soft whispers breeze, like morning dew.
Awakening our senses wide,
Filling hearts with warmest pride.

Mountains dance with shadows long,
Nature's chorus sings a song.
Horizons stretch, inviting us near,
In every moment, clear and dear.

We wander through this warm expanse,
In harmony, we find our dance.
With open hearts, we draw the day,
In every breath, we find our way.

As daylight fades, stars will peek,
The world is tender, calm and meek.
With every sunset, dreams transform,
In horizons bathed, we are reborn.

Paths of Glistening Possibility

Through glades of green our feet will tread,
Each path a story waiting to be read.
With every turn, a chance to find,
The glistening dreams that spark the mind.

Misty trails beneath the trees,
Carried softly on the breeze.
In every echo, whispers flow,
Of wonders waiting to bestow.

Banished doubts and heavy fears,
With open hearts, let joy draw near.
A world of colors, bright and bold,
Unfolding treasures yet untold.

In the distance, visions spark,
Guided by that shimmering arc.
We forge ahead, each step a dance,
Creating life with every chance.

Together on this journey grand,
With every wish, together we stand.
Paths of promise, vast and wide,
In glistening beauty, we confide.

Gentle Light Through the Charmed Clouds

Amidst the clouds, a soft embrace,
Gentle light breaks through in grace.
Casting shadows on the ground,
In every silence, joys abound.

The sky a canvas painted bright,
Illuminating dreams in flight.
Fleeting moments, captured fast,
In the charm of shadows cast.

With every ray that warms the soul,
We find the pieces that make us whole.
Through these whispers, spirits play,
In every dawn, a brand new day.

Let us bask in this golden hue,
As colors blend, each heart anew.
In this dance of light and shade,
A symphony of dreams is made.

So here we gather, hand in hand,
In gentle light, together we stand.
Through charmed clouds, our futures weave,
In every moment, we believe.

Splendor in the Quiet Morning

In dawn's embrace, the world awakes,
Soft whispers breathe where silence breaks.
The golden light, a gentle kiss,
Invites the heart to dance in bliss.

Birds sing sweetly in perfumed air,
Nature dons her jewels rare.
With each moment, calm resides,
In quietude, the spirit glides.

Gentle hues paint skies with grace,
As shadows flee from the sun's face.
A tranquil start, the day unfolds,
In splendor, every story told.

The dew upon the grass does gleam,
Like dreams reflected in a stream.
With every heartbeat, hope ignites,
In morning's glow, the soul takes flight.

In this stillness, life renews,
Wrapped in warmth and vibrant hues.
The quiet morning sings her song,
In splendor, where we all belong.

Echoes of a Faithful Sunrise

The sun peeks over hills so high,
A faithful friend who will not die.
With rays that cast away the night,
Awakening the world to light.

Each sunrise whispers soft and low,
A promise that we all can grow.
In hues of orange, pink, and gold,
A story of the brave retold.

Birds take wing in jubilant flight,
Celebrating morning's light.
The sky a canvas, bold and bright,
Painting dreams into the sight.

The warmth upon the eager earth,
Ushering in a brand-new birth.
With every rise, the heart can feel,
Embracing all that mornings heal.

In echoes of the day begun,
The harmony of life has spun.
A faithful sunrise, clear and true,
Reminds us all what hope can do.

Tapestries Woven with Dreams

In moonlit night, the stars align,
A tapestry, both yours and mine.
Threads of hope and wishes spun,
Under the gaze of a watching sun.

Colors blend in vibrant grace,
Each moment weaving time and space.
With dreams adorned in shimmering light,
Crafting stories that take to flight.

Whispers of what the heart desires,
Igniting deep, unquenchable fires.
With every stitch, a tale is told,
In woven depth, both bright and bold.

The fabric of our lives entwined,
In patterns rich, our fates defined.
Carried forth with gentle hands,
Creating worlds where love expands.

So let us weave our hopes anew,
In every shade, a spark to strew.
A tapestry that knows no seams,
Embracing all our cherished dreams.

Illuminated Moments of Anticipation

In quiet stillness, hearts await,
Illuminated paths of fate.
Each breath a thread of sweet desire,
Stirring embers, igniting fire.

The tick of time, a gentle guide,
With whispered secrets, dreams abide.
Every flicker, every spark,
A promise glowing in the dark.

In moments fragile, yet so bold,
Stories weave as time unfolds.
With every heartbeat, pulses race,
In anticipation's warm embrace.

The dawn approaches, soft and clear,
With every sigh, we draw it near.
Embracing hopes, we stand aligned,
In the dance of fate intertwined.

So let us savor each delight,
In illuminated paths so bright.
For every moment we will find,
The beauty of the heart and mind.

In Praise of Sun-Kissed Horizons

The sun rises gently, painting the sky,
With hues of gold and whispers of light.
Each day unfolds with a promise to try,
Embracing the warmth as day turns bright.

Waves of warmth grace our eager skin,
As laughter dances upon the breeze.
Underneath the vastness, we begin,
Finding joy in moments that aim to please.

Fields shimmer softly, kissed by the glow,
Where dreams take shape and the heart feels free.
In every shadow, a story does grow,
Written in colors of harmony.

With every sunset, we gather and sigh,
Thanking the sky for its dazzling show.
In praise we stand, letting worries fly,
As stars awaken to complement the flow.

So here's to horizons, so bright, so wide,
In their embrace, we find hope renewed.
With sun-kissed promises, we take the stride,
In the glow of tomorrow, our spirits viewed.

Blooming Light in the Anticipation

In the hush of twilight, whispers arise,
Petals unfurl under the watchful moon.
Hope takes root, held in nature's ties,
Opening hearts to a blooming tune.

Each morning beckons, a canvas to paint,
With colors of dreams and wishes anew.
A symphony formed, delicate yet quaint,
In every heartbeat, potential's in view.

Bright dewdrops shimmer, like jewels in grass,
Reflecting the light of a dawning day.
Through trials faced, moments shall pass,
In anticipation, we find our way.

The fragrance of blossoms fills the air,
With warmth of the sun on our grateful skin.
Beneath the vast sky, we shed every care,
And dance in the light as new journeys begin.

So let each moment be filled with delight,
As hopes bloom forth in the soft morning glow.
With hearts wide open, embrace the bright,
In the fabric of time, let love overflow.

The Essence of Tomorrow's Dawn

In shadows of night, dreams softly blend,
With whispers of hope that beckon the day.
Each dawn breaks open, tales without end,
Guiding our souls in a luminous way.

The horizon glows with colors profound,
Painting the world in hues yet untold.
With every sunrise, new stories abound,
And with every heartbeat, our futures unfold.

Gentle breezes carry the songs of the morn,
As nature awakens with a glorious cheer.
In every flower, a promise reborn,
Celebrating life with those we hold dear.

Together we stand, in radiant light,
Embracing the magic of moments so sweet.
With hearts intertwined, we face every fight,
Finding strength and courage in love's heartbeat.

So cherish each dawn and the essence it brings,
In the tapestry woven, our hopes shall soar.
For with every sunrise, potential still sings,
In the essence of life, we forever explore.

Whispers of a Dawn's Embrace

In the hush of morning's glow,
Soft whispers dance, a gentle flow.
The sky unfolds in shades so bright,
Awakening dreams with fleeting light.

Birds serenade the waking skies,
As shadows fade, the daylight flies.
Each petal glistens with the dew,
A tender kiss, the world anew.

The trees sway softly, tales untold,
In every breeze, a touch of gold.
The sun peeks through, a radiant smile,
Embracing life for a little while.

Through the meadows, the laughter flows,
Nature's heart in sweet repose.
In this moment, time stands still,
A cherished sigh, a gentle thrill.

As daylight blooms, we find our way,
In whispers sweet of dawn's ballet.
Each heartbeat sings a timeless song,
In the embrace where we belong.

Radiance Beyond the Horizon

Beyond the hills, the sun will rise,
Painting the world in brilliant ties.
A canvas bright with hues so bold,
Whispers of warmth as day unfolds.

Golden rays kiss the waking earth,
Igniting splendor, a joyful birth.
In the distance, shadows flee,
As light enshrouds the sleeping sea.

Clouds drift softly, a canvas vast,
Carrying dreams of futures cast.
Each moment shines with hopes embraced,
In the glow where love is chased.

Mountains echo with the dawn's sweet tune,
While the day sparkles beneath the moon.
Time dances lightly, a fleeting gleam,
In the radiance, we chase our dream.

Endless skies, in sapphire blue,
Hold the promise of something new.
With every step, we find our chance,
In the light, we share a trance.

A Canvas of Morning Light

Brushstrokes gold on the waking glaze,
Woven together in a morning daze.
Each color whispers, a tale untold,
In the warmth, a promise unfolds.

Softly the light spills on the trees,
In gentle caresses, a tender breeze.
Nature awakens, a symphony rings,
As the day shares the joy it brings.

Shimmering streams reflect the sun,
Carrying secrets of all that's begun.
With every ripple, a story flows,
In the dance where tranquility grows.

Petals open, their beauty so rare,
Filling the world with fragrant air.
In the hush, where silence sings,
We became part of the magic it brings.

All around, life starts to ignite,
In the heart of a canvas, pure light.
With hopes alight, we rise and soar,
Embracing the art of what's in store.

Shimmering Dreams in Celestial Blue

In the deep of night, stars brightly play,
Casting their wishes, lighting the way.
A cosmic dance in a velvet sky,
Where shimmering dreams learn to fly.

Moonlit whispers caress the land,
As dreams unfold, gentle and grand.
Each twinkle holds a secret untold,
In the heart of the night, stories unfold.

Time drifts softly on a silver stream,
Where every thought is a fleeting dream.
The universe listens, embracing our sighs,
Connecting souls in magical ties.

A tapestry woven with silver thread,
Threads of hopes and things left unsaid.
With every breath, we touch the divine,
In celestial realms where stars entwine.

As dawn approaches, the dreams will blend,
With a gentle heart, we start to mend.
In shimmering moments, the night will flee,
But the echoes of dreams will always be free.

Gentle Promises in Cascading Hues

In twilight's soft embrace we find,
Whispers of dreams so sweetly aligned.
Colors dance across the sky,
As evening sighs, its lullaby.

Petals fall like fleeting time,
A promise held in each soft rhyme.
Through shadows deep, a spark remains,
In every heart, love's gentle gains.

The rivers glimmer with fading light,
Painting tales of day and night.
In each reflection, truth unfolds,
Of stories whispered, yet untold.

Moonlit breezes softly sway,
Guiding lost souls on their way.
With every star that begins to gleam,
A gentle promise, a shared dream.

The Resurgence of Light's Lament

From shadows deep where silence waits,
A flicker sparks, as night abates.
Through weeping clouds, a silver line,
Awakens hearts to dreams divine.

Each teardrop falls, a tale of grace,
Reflecting hope in dark's embrace.
As dawn breaks forth, the night shall yield,
To whispers bright, the heart is healed.

The weary stones, they softly sigh,
In cracks and crevices, joy will lie.
With every note of nature's song,
The light returns, where souls belong.

So let the candle's flame ignite,
The path ahead, through darkest night.
For every shadow, light will mend,
And in this dance, our hearts ascend.

Beyond the Veil, a New Day Awaits

Behind the veil where shadows play,
A whispered hope greets each new day.
With every dawn, the past will fade,
A canvas fresh, where dreams are laid.

Through morning mist, the world awakes,
In gentle hues, the silence breaks.
With vibrant strokes, the sun will rise,
To paint the skies, a sweet surprise.

In the stillness, hearts will yearn,
For each new twist, each vibrant turn.
Beyond the veil, horizons call,
To forge a path, to rise, to fall.

As daylight dances on the streams,
The whispers weave through waking dreams.
Each moment precious, none in vain,
In life's embrace, we break our chains.

Horizons Spun with Silver Threads

Horizons stretch with quiet grace,
Each silver thread a soft embrace.
In twilight's glow, a journey starts,
We weave our hopes, we share our hearts.

The stars above, they gently shine,
As dreams intertwine, your hand in mine.
With every heartbeat, stories flow,
In whispered winds, our spirits grow.

Across the seas, the world unfolds,
In tangled paths, adventure holds.
With every dawn, the canvas grows,
A tapestry where passion glows.

Through valleys deep and mountains high,
The silver threads forever tie.
In love and laughter, we transcend,
For on this journey, we shall mend.

Celestial Serenity Paints the Day

In morning's glow, the heavens sigh,
A canvas brushed in softest hue,
Whispers of dawn, as dreams float by,
Each moment new, a gift in view.

The clouds drift gently, light they weave,
A symphony of colors blend,
In silence deep, we cease to grieve,
As nature's art, our hearts commend.

The sun ascends with golden rays,
Through branches dancing, shadows play,
In peace we find our secret ways,
Celestial guidance, night turns day.

With every breath, the world awakes,
A tapestry dressed fresh and bright,
In splendor vast, the spirit shakes,
Celestial grace, our inner light.

So let us wander, hand in hand,
Through painted skies, our souls will sing,
In unity, together stand,
As love's embrace makes the heart spring.

Radiant Paths to Tomorrow

With every step, the journey starts,
A winding road of hopes and dreams,
Through shadows cast, yet brave our hearts,
Together we'll find brighter beams.

The sunrise beckons, colors flare,
Each path unfolds with stories sworn,
In faith we trust, a life to share,
For every end brings a new dawn.

Through storms we tread, with heads held high,
In trials faced, our spirits grow,
The future calls, with wings to fly,
In radiant light, our strength we show.

Each moment shared, a treasure spun,
In laughter rich, our fears dissolve,
The world's a stage, our dance begun,
With dreams aflame, our hearts evolve.

So here's to what is yet to find,
The paths that lead to tomorrow's grace,
With courage bold, our souls aligned,
Our journey blooms in love's embrace.

A Prelude of Brilliant Futures

In twilight's glow, the dreams ignite,
A canvas stretched for all to see,
Each stroke of fate, a spark of light,
A prelude rich, where hope runs free.

With stars alight, ambitions soar,
Through whispered winds, our hearts take flight,
In unity, we seek for more,
A brilliant path, our guiding light.

Through trials faced, we find our voice,
In every heartbeat, strength emerges,
Together still, we make the choice,
To strive for all our soul encourages.

With every dream, the night unfolds,
A tapestry of endless stars,
In faith and love, our spirit holds,
A prelude bright, no fate of ours.

So let us rise, embrace the dawn,
With open eyes to futures bright,
In every moment, draw upon,
The path that leads us to the light.

Enveloping Light After the Storm

The storm has passed, the sky now clears,
In hues of blue and softest gold,
With every drop, we shed our fears,
As nature's breath, our hearts unfold.

In gentle rays, the earth awakes,
A symphony of peace returns,
With every smile, the spirit shakes,
In warmth embraced, our passion burns.

The air is fresh, like life anew,
With fragrant blooms that kiss the ground,
In harmony, the world's a view,
Where hope resides, and joy is found.

Together here, we stand in grace,
In light that dances, shadows flee,
The past is gone, a new embrace,
Enveloping warmth, we're truly free.

So linger long, in this bright hour,
For love and light are always near,
With hearts entwined, we share our power,
Enveloping light, a bond sincere.

The Heartbeat of Rising Sunlight

In the hush before dawn's first call,
Shadows linger, somber and small.
A whisper stirs the quiet air,
Awakening dreams beyond compare.

Golden rays break the night's hold,
Painting horizons with strokes of gold.
Each pulse a promise, bright and bold,
Embracing the warmth, as tales unfold.

Nature's choir joins in the light,
Celebrating the end of night.
With every heartbeat, the world sings,
Welcoming joy that morning brings.

The sky blushes in hues of flame,
A tribute to life, none could tame.
In the glory of dawn's embrace,
Hope finds a home in this sacred space.

As shadows flee, the spirit soars,
Heartbeats echo on distant shores.
We dance with the dawn, fresh and free,
In the heartbeat of sunlight, we find our glee.

Colors of Courage in the Sky

Glimmers of crimson rise on high,
Filling hearts as shadows fly.
Each hue a story, bold and bright,
Whispering courage, igniting the light.

Azure waves in the peaceful breeze,
Carrying dreams with effortless ease.
Golden streaks of bravery show,
In every heart, a fire to grow.

Violet echoes of twilight's dance,
Emboldening souls through every chance.
With colors alive in radiant sprawl,
Together we stand, united, tall.

Emerald hopes stretch across the land,
In vibrant beauty, we take a stand.
Each brushstroke of light tells a tale,
Of courage born, where dreams prevail.

Underneath this vast canvas wide,
We paint our futures, side by side.
In the colors of courage, we trust,
To forge a path, bright and robust.

Embracing the Soft Light of Tomorrow

Morning dew on petals, so bright,
Whispering secrets in soft light.
Each moment cradles a gentle sigh,
As dreams unfold beneath the sky.

With every breath, we release the past,
Inviting new blessings, unsurpassed.
The dawn wraps us in its warm embrace,
A promise of hope, a sacred space.

Tender rays bathe the waking earth,
Bearing gifts of love and rebirth.
With courage, we step into the day,
Embracing the light in every way.

Clouds drift softly like thoughts in flight,
Carrying wishes to new heights.
In the stillness, we find our way,
Guided by the soft light of day.

As shadows fade and worries cease,
We gather strength, we find our peace.
In the tender glow of tomorrow's rise,
Hope blooms anew, under open skies.

Veils of Hope in Amber Hues

Twilight drapes in amber grace,
Painting dreams in a warm embrace.
Each veil a whisper of light anew,
In the stillness, hope breaks through.

Soft reflections on the water's face,
Mirroring moments that time won't chase.
With every ripple, the heart beats strong,
In the tapestry of life, we belong.

As day meets night in a gentle sway,
Courage blooms as doubts decay.
Radiant threads weave through the air,
Uniting souls in a dance so rare.

With each breath, we harness the glow,
Embracing dreams that ebb and flow.
In the amber twilight, we find our way,
Where hope's sweet fragrance forever stays.

Veils of love wrap us tight,
Guiding hearts into the night.
In the soft hues where shadows play,
Hope beckons gently, come what may.

Beyond the Clouds of Yesterday

In the sky where lost dreams drift,
Memories sigh, in silence they shift.
Whispers dance on the cool, soft breeze,
Time lingers still, wrapped in sweet ease.

Through the haze, a new day beckons,
Chance to heal, as the heart reckons.
Fleeting shadows start to part ways,
Leaving behind the darker days.

With each ray, old sorrows recede,
Hope unfolds like a blooming seed.
Trust the journey, uncharted space,
Embrace the light in time and place.

The canvas brightens, colors entwine,
Paint your story, let your heart shine.
Beyond the clouds, horizons stretch far,
Beneath the sun, find who you are.

So rise with the dawn, let the past fade,
In the warmth of the light, be unafraid.
Through the clouds, find your truth anew,
Beyond the shadows, skies ever blue.

Shadows Banish with Dawn's Arrival

As the night whispers its last goodbyes,
The sun climbs high in the vast, bright skies.
Shadows linger, yet slowly retreat,
Illuminated by day's warm heartbeat.

With each ray, hope begins to swell,
Breaking the silence where darkness fell.
Colors awaken, life starts to sing,
The joy of dawn, what a gift it brings.

Each moment glimmers, fresh and alive,
In the light, weary souls start to thrive.
Lost dreams now glisten like dew on the grass,
Eclipsed by the light, only shadows shall pass.

Feel the warmth of the morning's embrace,
Banish the doubts, find your own pace.
Take a step forward, let worries be few,
In the dance of the dawn, find strength that is true.

Shadows dissolve, and the world appears,
In the glow of promise, conquer your fears.
Let the sunrise be your guiding star,
Shadows banished, you've come so far.

Horizons Awash in Hopeful Tides

At the edge of the sea, the daylight breaks,
Waves whisper love, the world gently shakes.
Horizons awaken, painted with gold,
Stories of hope and dreams yet untold.

The vast blue stretches, a canvas so wide,
Carrying wishes on the rhythmic tide.
Each gentle wave brings a vision anew,
The future awaits, all it needs is you.

Seagulls soar high, embracing the breeze,
In their flight lies the joy of the seas.
With every heartbeat, the promise grows bolder,
Steps taken forward, the weight grows so much colder.

Feel the pull of the water and sand,
The dance of the tides is serenely planned.
Let the waves guide your heart on this ride,
Trust in the journey, let hope be your guide.

As the day stretches forth into view,
Awash in colors, embrace what is true.
Horizons alive, let your spirit be wide,
Reach for the dreams in the ebb of the tide.

Emblems of Tomorrow in Morning's Glow

Underneath the brightening sky,
Ashes of old hopes begin to fly.
Morning's glow, a gentle embrace,
Carrying dreams to a brighter place.

Each dawn paints a future, fresh and bold,
In the whispers of light, stories unfold.
The heart beats in rhythm with each new day,
In the warmth of the sun, doubts drift away.

With each step forward, find what you seek,
In the freedom of morning, the spirit won't speak.
Stars of the night fade one by one,
All that remains is the promise of sun.

Hold close the visions of all that is near,
In the morning's embrace, passion appears.
Emblems of tomorrow bloom in the light,
Guiding us forward from darkness to bright.

So rise with the sun, let dreams take their flight,
In the glow of the day, the future feels right.
Together we stand, under skies that will show,
Emblems of hope in morning's soft glow.

Murmurs of Joy Cresting the Day

The sun peeks over the hill,
Whispers of light start to spill.
Birds sing sweet, a gentle cheer,
Morning breaks, the joy is clear.

Dewdrops glisten on the grass,
Moments like this will always pass.
Yet in the warmth, we find our stay,
Murmurs of joy cresting the day.

A breeze carries laughter's tune,
Softly dancing with the moon.
Each heartbeat thrives in this embrace,
Life unfolds, a wondrous space.

Colors blend with every sigh,
As hearts lift up, they learn to fly.
Hope is born with every ray,
Murmurs of joy cresting the day.

As shadows fade into the light,
We carry forth this sweet delight.
In every smile, a silent play,
Murmurs of joy cresting the day.

A Skyline Unfurled in Color

The sky ignites with hues so bright,
A canvas painted day and night.
Clouds drift by in shades so bold,
Stories of wonder waiting to be told.

With every dawn, the colors swell,
In soft whispers, they weave a spell.
Cascading tones of pink and gold,
A skyline unfurled, a beauty to behold.

As twilight fades, the stars come alive,
In this tapestry, dreams arrive.
An echo of twilight's warm embrace,
A moment captured, time and space.

From dusk till dawn, the colors blend,
Nature's artistry, a timeless trend.
Underneath this vast display,
A skyline unfurled in color, we stay.

In every brush stroke, a heartbeat sings,
Joy and wonder in simple things.
We breathe in deep, life's vibrant play,
A skyline unfurled in color, we sway.

Reflections of a Brighter Path

Footprints mark the winding way,
Each step taken, a choice to sway.
Sunshine dances on the ground,
In each moment, hope is found.

Ripples echo through the stream,
Carrying along each dream.
Shadows whisper from the past,
Yet brighter futures are cast.

With courage, we can face the night,
Finding strength in inner light.
Together, hands entwined, we start,
Reflections of a brighter heart.

Every challenge helps us grow,
In kindness, love begins to flow.
Like blossoms blooming in the May,
Reflections of a brighter path, we lay.

The sky will turn, the seasons shift,
Yet in our hearts, the love will lift.
With every breath, we find our way,
Reflections of a brighter path, we stay.

Embracing the Soft Hues of Delight

In twilight's glow, the world is still,
Gentle whispers, a peaceful thrill.
Colors wrap around the night,
Embracing soft hues, pure delight.

The stars twinkle like distant dreams,
Filling the air with silver beams.
Each heartbeat syncs with nature's song,
In this moment, we belong.

With every sigh, serenity flows,
As tranquil twilight slowly grows.
A dance of shadows, soft and light,
Embracing the soft hues of delight.

In laughter shared, true joy we find,
The wonder in each heart aligned.
Lost in the beauty, nothing feels wrong,
Embracing the soft hues, we sing along.

Through softest whispers, love ignites,
A canvas painted on starry nights.
Holding tight, as dreams take flight,
Embracing the soft hues of delight.

Shining Beacons of Tomorrow's Heart

In the dawn's gentle light, they rise,
Hope glimmering in their eyes.
Each step forward, a story unfolds,
Braving the storms, bold and gold.

Dreams weave through the silken air,
Stronger are those who dare.
With every pulse, their hearts ignite,
Guiding the lost through the night.

Whispers of courage fill the skies,
As doubts fade and bravery flies.
Together they stand, hand in hand,
Building a future, a brighter land.

Rays of promise flicker above,
Illuminating paths of love.
In unity, their spirits soar,
Echoing hopes forevermore.

So let them shine, these beacons bright,
Leading our dreams into the light.
For in their glow, we find our way,
Shining together, come what may.

Tints of Courage on the Water's Edge

On the shore where waves do play,
Colors dance in bright array.
Each hue tells tales of brave hearts,
Marking where a journey starts.

Sunsets drape the ocean wide,
With whispers of the rising tide.
In each ripple, courage glows,
As relentless spirit grows.

Reflections shimmer, dreams awake,
Reflecting choices that we make.
Guiding sailors through the night,
With hopes that burn, fierce and bright.

In the breeze, a soft lament,
For all the paths that courage lent.
Every heart that dares to strive,
Ignites the world and keeps it alive.

So on the water's edge we stand,
With colors vivid, hand in hand.
Embracing the courage we hold dear,
Transforming doubt into cheer.

A Symphony of Lights and Dreams

In the night, the stars align,
Crafting a dance, pure and divine.
Each light a note in a cosmic score,
Whispering dreams of so much more.

As melodies rise, thoughts take flight,
Filling the sky with hope's delight.
With every twinkle, a chance to be,
A symphony of hearts set free.

Echoes of wishes float through air,
Binding souls in a tapestry rare.
With every beat, life's rhythm plays,
Guiding us through the intricate maze.

Each dream ignites a spark so bright,
Creating shadows that dance in the night.
Together we weave our tales anew,
In a world adorned with dreams come true.

So let the music lead the way,
As hopes illuminate night and day.
In this symphony, we find our voice,
In light and dreams, we rejoice.

Sailing on the Wings of Dawn

With each sunrise, a new begin,
Sailing forth on dreams within.
The horizon calls, bold and bright,
Guided by the morning light.

Waves of promise gently sway,
Carrying hearts that long to play.
As whispers cross the ocean's face,
We chase our hopes at our own pace.

Tales unfold on the salty breeze,
Nurturing desires that aim to please.
With every gust, we scream our dreams,
Riding life's wild, vibrant streams.

In the distance, a promise glows,
A reminder of where the heart goes.
Together we chart our course anew,
Sailing on the winds so true.

So set your sails, embrace the dawn,
With courage as our lifelong bond.
In every wave, our spirits rise,
Sailing freely, touching skies.

Dawn's Chorus in Blushing Tints

The sun peeks through the veil of night,
Soft pinks and golds embrace the sight.
Birds awaken, singing sweet,
Nature's symphony, a morning greet.

Whispers of light begin to play,
Chasing the shadows, leading the way.
Each note a promise, fresh and clear,
In dawn's chorus, hope draws near.

Gentle breezes carry the song,
Inviting all to sing along.
With every breath, a brand new chance,
In blushing tints, the day's romance.

Clouds blush softly, touched with fire,
As day unfolds with sweet desire.
Within the glow, our dreams ignite,
Painting the heavens with pure delight.

Let the dawn's embrace enfold our hearts,
In every corner, beauty imparts.
Together we rise, hand in hand,
In harmony with this vibrant land.

Luminous Wishes on the Wind

Wishes travel with the breeze,
Dancing lightly through the trees.
Each whisper carries dreams anew,
A canvas painted with skies so blue.

Beneath the stars, our hopes take flight,
Fleeting moments in the night.
Gentle sighs of longing start,
As luminous thoughts fill every heart.

With every gust, they weave and twirl,
Spinning softly, like a pearl.
They touch the corners of the earth,
Bearing tales of love and mirth.

As silver threads in twilight's glow,
Wishes flourish; they ebb and flow.
They bridge the gaps between our souls,
Binding us with unbroken rolls.

So let them soar on winds so free,
A symphony of dreams to see.
We hold our hearts, let them ascend,
In luminous wishes, love transcends.

Celestial Flames of Aspiration

Stars ignite in the velvet night,
A cosmic canvas, pure delight.
Each point of light, a dream so bright,
Celestial flames, our hearts take flight.

With every flicker, a path revealed,
To desires buried, now unsealed.
We reach across the vast unknown,
In unity, together we've grown.

Galaxies spin with tales to share,
Of courage found in moments rare.
In the darkness, our spirits gleam,
In celestial flames, we dare to dream.

Radiant embers spark our will,
In courage's grip, our hearts we fill.
No mountain too high, no sea too wide,
In aspirations, we shall abide.

With every breath, we climb anew,
To realms of hope, where wishes brew.
In cosmic dance, our spirits soar,
Celestial flames, we seek for more.

When Daybreak Dances

When daybreak dances on the sky,
Golden rays that reach so high.
Every hue, a chance to gleam,
Awakening life like a dream.

Fleeting moments of morning light,
Whispers soft, a pure delight.
Nature stirs, the world takes wing,
In gentle rhythms, hearts will sing.

With every beam, shadows retreat,
The day unfurls, life feels sweet.
Embrace the warmth, let laughter flow,
In daybreak's dance, our spirits grow.

The canvas brightens, colors blend,
With every breath, let worries end.
In harmony, the dawn unfolds,
A tale of hope that nature holds.

So gather close and feel the grace,
As daybreak dances, find your place.
In this embrace, the world renews,
With golden dreams and morning dews.

A Canvas Bright with Possibility

Before the dawn, a canvas waits,
Colors blend, where hope elates.
Brushstrokes whisper dreams anew,
Life unfolds in every hue.

A palette rich with untold schemes,
Crafting visions, weaving dreams.
Each stroke a story yet to shine,
In this space, all is divine.

The sun will rise on blank expanse,
Awakening a vibrant dance.
With every shade, a tale ignites,
In this canvas, pure delights.

A symphony of sights and sounds,
Where every heartbeat knows the grounds.
In strokes of truth, our spirits fly,
Colors painted, reaching high.

So let the brush in freedom play,
Creating worlds, come what may.
With every mark, we dare to dream,
A canvas bright, a joyful theme.

Illuminated Paths of Destiny

Along the way, the lanterns glow,
Shadows dance with whispers low.
Footsteps echo on the ground,
In the night, our paths are found.

Each step a choice, a turn to take,
Veering close to life's great wake.
By guiding lights, our fates align,
In the darkness, stars will shine.

Moments flicker like candle flames,
Offering solace, calling names.
Truths unfold as journeys blend,
At the journey's heart, we mend.

With courage, we embrace our fate,
Choosing joy, not fear or hate.
The road ahead may twist and wind,
But every path the heart can find.

In the glow of dreams and plans,
We walk the line where courage stands.
Forever bound to destiny,
Illuminated paths, we see.

Colors of an Unseen Sunrise

In the stillness, dawn awaits,
Painting skies with vibrant rates.
Each hue a promise, soft and bright,
Revealing worlds lost to the night.

Brush the clouds with tender glow,
Where dreams take flight and spirits grow.
In whispers, the colors intertwine,
Creating warmth, transcending time.

The earth awakens, gently stirred,
Hushed visions voiced without a word.
Golden rays caress the morn,
Inviting life where hope is born.

With every shade, a tale unfolds,
In nature's lap, a heart consoled.
Hidden wonders find their way,
In the dance of light, we stay.

So let us breathe this beauty in,
As day anew is set to begin.
In unseen sun, our hearts arise,
For life awaits in painted skies.

Echoes of Resilience

In the silence, whispers hum,
Tales of strength, the overcoming drum.
From the ashes, spirits rise,
Courage gleams in weary eyes.

Every fall, a lesson learned,
Through the struggle, hearts have burned.
In the face of fear, we stand,
Building castles from the sand.

With every heartbeat, stories sway,
Against the night, we find our way.
Through storms endured, we stand tall,
In the echoes, hear the call.

Resilience paints the path we tread,
With scars of honor, we're led.
In the darkest night, hope can bloom,
Filling hearts, dispelling gloom.

So let us rise with strength imbued,
In unity, our voices glued.
Together, we'll face the dawn's new light,
Echoes of resilience, fierce and bright.

Whispers of Dawn's Embrace

In the hush, the dawn breaks bright,
Colors dance in fading night.
Softly glows the world anew,
As whispers drift, a gentle hue.

Sunrise paints the skies with gold,
Stories of the night retold.
Gentle breezes begin to sway,
Embracing hope in the new day.

Morning dew on petals lies,
The sweetness of a soft surprise.
Nature stirs from dreams so deep,
In every heart, a promise keeps.

Birds take flight in joyous song,
Their melodies where they belong.
With each note, the world awakes,
In this moment, a love transcends.

Here in stillness, peace we find,
Hearts intertwined, two souls aligned.
In whispers soft, the dawn reveals,
A tenderness that gently heals.

Light Beyond the Storm

Through the clouds, the thunder rolls,
Echoes loud in weary souls.
Yet within this raging plight,
There flickers still a distant light.

Waves may crash and shadows loom,
But hope can pierce the deepest gloom.
In the heart, a fire glows,
Guiding through what darkness throws.

Raindrops fall like whispered dreams,
Each one holds a promise, it seems.
Soon the sun will break the gray,
Painting skies in bright array.

When the winds begin to cease,
In their wake, we find our peace.
From the struggle, strength is born,
We rise anew, each soul reborn.

So here we stand, hand in hand,
Facing storms, we make our stand.
For after trials, love will bloom,
Lighting paths beyond the gloom.

Keep the faith, let courage swell,
In every heart, a story to tell.
Through the chaos, find your song,
In the light, together we belong.

When Stars Begin to Sing

In the velvet of the night,
Stars awaken, shining bright.
With a twinkle, they align,
Whispers soft, their dreams entwine.

As the moon begins to glow,
Melodies in silence flow.
Each note a distant memory,
Cradled in the galaxy.

Across the skies, a lullaby,
Every twinkle, a gentle sigh.
Wrapped in light, heartbeats dance,
In the night, a cosmic trance.

Listen close, oh wanderer,
To the tales they echo pure.
For in starlight, love's refrain,
Brings the soul a sweet sustain.

When horizons fade away,
Questions pause, the heart will play.
In that moment, silence hums,
When stars begin, love softly comes.

A Palette of Promise

Brush in hand, the canvas waits,
Colors whisper of our fates.
Strokes of hope, vivid and true,
Every hue, a tale anew.

From deep blues to bright romance,
Each shade holds a fleeting chance.
A splash of red for love's bold grace,
The quiet greens of nature's embrace.

In every color, dreams ignite,
Painting worlds both day and night.
With every layer, hearts unfold,
In this voyage, stories told.

Golden yellows, warmth and light,
Guide us through the darkest night.
In this palette, hope remains,
Filling spaces with sweet refrains.

So dip your brush, let courage soar,
In this art, you'll find your core.
For in creation, life's design,
A promise made, forever shine.

Hope's Radiant Afterglow

In the quiet dusk, dreams take flight,
Whispers of courage kiss the night.
Stars awaken, soft and bright,
Hope's embrace ignites the light.

Each heart beats with a warm desire,
Casting shadows, setting fire.
Through the dark, we aspire,
Together we'll rise, lifting higher.

The world unfolds, a canvas wide,
With colors bold, and hearts as guides.
We walk with faith, side by side,
In hope's warm glow, we'll abide.

Amidst the storms, we find our way,
Holding on to dreams that sway.
With every dawn, we dare to play,
In hope's embrace, we'll never stray.

What lies ahead, we cannot know,
Yet in our hearts, a gentle glow.
For every end, there's room to grow,
In hope's radiant afterglow.

Luminescence at Daybreak

As dawn creeps in, the world ignites,
Gold and amber take their flights.
Whispers of dawn in soft delights,
Painting skies with radiant sights.

Each ray a promise, pure and clear,
Chasing shadows far and near.
Hope awakes within our sphere,
With every heartbeat, love draws near.

Through the mist, the light cascades,
In its warmth, our worries fade.
A gentle kiss, the sun parades,
In luminescence, joy invades.

Birds take wing, a soaring flight,
Beneath the vast expanse of light.
With every note, the heart takes flight,
In symphonies of day's delight.

As colors blend, the world awakes,
Boundless dreams, the dawn remakes.
In every heart, a hope that stakes,
In luminescence, life partakes.

Beyond the Clouds of Tomorrow

In twilight's glow, the future waits,
Beyond the clouds, where hope translates.
A gentle breeze, the night elates,
With dreams that dance through open gates.

Stars align in patterns bright,
Guiding souls through the night.
In shadows long, our hearts take flight,
Beyond the clouds, we find our light.

Each moment shared, a spark so bold,
In tales of warmth, our hearts unfold.
Through trials faced, and stories told,
Together we brave, with spirits gold.

The dawn approaches, soft and sweet,
Where dreams and reality meet.
In every heartbeat, love's heartbeat,
Beyond the clouds, life feels complete.

With faith as our guide, we journey on,
In the embrace of dusk and dawn.
With every step, new hope is drawn,
Beyond the clouds of tomorrow, we con.

A Symphony of Celestial Hues

Night unfolds with a whispered song,
Stars composed, where they belong.
In shades of blue, the world feels strong,
A symphony of hues, where dreams prolong.

Moonlight weaves through branches bare,
Guiding hearts, with tender care.
In silence felt, a prayer laid bare,
In celestial nights, love fills the air.

Through every color, wishes rise,
With twinkling stars as faithful ties.
In the dance of light, hope never dies,
A symphony sung beneath the skies.

Each note a heartbeat, pure and true,
Resonating with skies of blue.
Together we dream, creating new,
In a symphony of celestial hues.

As dawn approaches with golden threads,
The music whispers, softly spreads.
In every heart, the dream is fed,
A symphony of life, where love is led.

Shimmering Reflections of Belief

In the mirror of the soul, we gaze,
Crowns of dreams in the morning haze.
Faith flickers, a candle's bright light,
Guiding us through the depth of night.

Waves of hope on a tranquil sea,
Whispers of love, set our hearts free.
Every tear, a crystal aglow,
Sows a garden where courage may grow.

Through shadows we wander, yet still we rise,
Painting our futures across open skies.
With every step, a promise to keep,
Shimmering reflections in silence deep.

Hand in hand, we walk this fine line,
Where thoughts converge and destinies shine.
In the tapestry woven, so rich and bright,
We find our strength in the warmth of light.

Let the tapestry of belief unfurl,
In each heart, a universe to swirl.
Together we stand, with dreams in reach,
In shimmering reflections, love will teach.

The Song of Awakening Skies

Dawn breaks softly, a gentle sigh,
Colors awaken, painting the sky.
Birdsong swells in the cool air,
A melody blooms, everywhere.

Clouds drift lazily, white on blue,
Each note a promise of something new.
With every rise of the golden sun,
Harmony lingers, our hearts are one.

Nature's chorus, a heartfelt tune,
Rising with warmth from the brightening moon.
Life emerges from the silent night,
In the song of awakening, feel the light.

Breezes carry the whispers of dreams,
Filling our spirits with life's vivid schemes.
Every heartbeat, a rhythmic phrase,
In the song of the skies, we find our ways.

Together we dance to the cosmic beat,
In nature's embrace, our souls meet.
With each new dawn, our hopes arise,
Singing along with the awakening skies.

Daylight's Gentle Brushstrokes

Morning light spills over the hills,
Painting the world with soft, warm thrills.
Each blade of grass, a canvas anew,
Touched by the sun's tender hue.

Shadows retreat from the day's embrace,
As daylight draws close, we quicken our pace.
The flowers bloom in vibrancy bright,
In the harmony born from the light.

Fingers of gold brush over the trees,
Whispering secrets in every breeze.
Nature smiles as it wakes from the night,
In daylight's embrace, all feels right.

Artistry flows in each radiant ray,
Strokes of life brightening the day.
A masterpiece crafted by time and grace,
In daylight's gentle touch, we find our place.

With every moment the sun's embrace,
Colors entwine in a loving trace.
Daylight dances, our hearts will sing,
In the brushstrokes of hope that spring.

The Dance of Graceful Light

Watch the shadows, they sway and bend,
As light begins its playful trend.
Twinkles of joy in a soft ballet,
In the dance of light, we find our way.

Silver beams glide on waves of gold,
Stories of old in their shimmer behold.
Each flicker and flash tells a tale so bright,
Guiding our path in the dark of night.

The moon dips down for a gentle kiss,
In twilight's embrace, we find our bliss.
Stars take flight on a waltz through the sky,
Reminding us softly, as moments pass by.

Light bends through branches, casting a spell,
A wondrous performance we know all too well.
In every twirl, a heartbeat, a spark,
Illuminating dreams within the dark.

Hold on to the dance, let it soar high,
In the rhythm of life, let your spirit fly.
With each shining hour, we take our part,
In the dance of graceful light, joy will start.

A Pallor of Promise in the Sky

Soft whispers of dawn, colors awake,
The horizon blushes, a pact we will make.
Clouds carry secrets, in shades of soft gray,
A pallor of promise, the birth of the day.

Gentle winds dance, with a tender caress,
The world holds its breath, in a moment of press.
Fingers of sunlight reach out from the mist,
Painting new dreams in a world filled with bliss.

Birds sing sweet verses, heralding hope,
On air thick with magic, our spirits elope.
Awake to the wonders, let worries take flight,
In this moment of promise, all shadows feel light.

A canvas of azure, the sky stretching wide,
The palette of life where our dreams can reside.
Embrace the soft glow as it warms every heart,
In the pallor of promise, a beautiful start.

Here in this twilight, where shadows may cling,
We rise with the light, and in unison sing.
Each note a reminder, as new dreams will fly,
In the quiet of dawn, a pallor of sky.

Stars that Fade to New Beginnings

In the hush of night, the stars start to fade,
Whispers of dawn, in soft colors displayed.
Each twinkle a promise, a wish in the dark,
Guiding our hearts towards a new, brighter arc.

The moon drapes her glow over quiet hills,
While dreams linger on, as the silence fulfills.
Time wrapped in starlight, where hope intertwines,
A tapestry woven with infinite lines.

But soon comes the light, breaking softly the veil,
With warmth that awakens, the world starts to sail.
Each moment a story, anew to be spun,
As stars slip to shadows and herald the sun.

In the soft morning glow, all fears are set free,
New beginnings arise with the promise to see.
The echoes of starlight still twinkle in mind,
In the warmth of the day, true magic we find.

Celebrate the dawn as the stars bid goodbye,
For endings bring forth what in time we reply.
A chapter unwritten, with colors so bold,
As stars fade to mornings, new dreams to behold.

The Quiet Assurance of Daylight

In the stillness of night, doubts often creep,
But daylight arrives, bringing comfort so deep.
Soft rays will uncover what shadows enclose,
The quiet assurance of how daylight flows.

Each beam is a promise, a gentle embrace,
Washing away fears, giving hope a new space.
Morning light glimmers, on petals it lies,
A sanctuary found in the brightening skies.

With every soft whisper, the world stirs awake,
The heartbeat of nature, a new day to make.
In colors reimagined, our spirits ascend,
The quiet assurance, as light will transcend.

Let shadows be fleeting, let doubts fall away,
For daylight is here, bringing joy to the day.
It's a canvas of beauty, a love we can trace,
In the arms of the daylight, we flourish with grace.

So welcome the light, for it's filled with sweet cheer,
In the quiet assurance, we have nothing to fear.
With hearts open wide, we reclaim our own way,
In the stillness of morning, we find our own say.

Tides of Light in a Sea of Dreams

In a sea of dreams, the tides gently sway,
Waves of soft light guide our fears far away.
With currents that whisper of moments so bright,
We drift on the waters, bathed in pure light.

Shadows may linger, but they soon will retreat,
As dawn paints the canvas where day and night meet.
Each ripple a promise, each splash a new chance,
In tides of soft brilliance, our spirits will dance.

The horizon beckons, where colors ignite,
With horizons that shimmer in the gentle twilight.
Embrace the adventure, let worries subside,
In the sea of our dreams, let our hopes be our guide.

As the sun dips below, a farewell to gray,
We welcome the night but in dreams we will stay.
The tides of our visions, forever will flow,
In the sea of our dreams, where magic will grow.

So sail through the night, and let love be your helm,
In a sea of light's shimmer, where dreams overwhelm.
In this ocean of wonder, make wishes take flight,
With tides of soft whispers, we cherish the night.

Unveiling Radiance in the Mellow Morn

In gentle hues, the dawn appears,
Soft whispers chase away the fears.
Golden beams through branches weave,
Embrace the light, let's not deceive.

The world awakes with a tender grace,
Every shadow, a warm embrace.
Nature sings a sweet refrain,
In waking dreams, we find our gain.

The morning dew, a jeweled sight,
Cascades down leaves, pure and bright.
With every drop, a story flows,
In tranquil moments, wonder grows.

As sunlight dances on the ground,
Awakening life, a joyful sound.
Birds arise with songs to share,
In this paradise, we all find care.

So let us greet this vital morn,
In every heart, the hope is born.
The day unfurls, a canvas wide,
With radiant light, our dreams abide.

A Journey into Daylight's Embrace

Step into the warmth of day,
The dawn invites us, come and play.
Whispers of the waking breeze,
Guide our souls with gentle ease.

Sunlight breaks through morning mist,
Inviting moments not to miss.
Every ray a tender touch,
Embracing all who seek so much.

Fields of gold and skies so blue,
A symphony of vibrant hue.
In every corner, joys align,
A sacred dance, a day divine.

Together we chase the fleeting light,
With open hearts, we embrace the sight.
Hand in hand, through fields we roam,
In this bright world, we make our home.

The sunlight guides us, ever bold,
Chasing dreams, both new and old.
With every step, we journey on,
United under a sky reborn.

Blossoms of Hope Adorning the Sky

In the garden where dreams reside,
Petals open, arms spread wide.
Colors blend in harmony,
Each bloom sings of joy, so free.

Hope emerges in every bud,
Rising gently from the mud.
Each bloom a promise, bright and clear,
Reminding us that love is near.

As butterflies begin to dance,
In sunlight's glow, they take the chance.
Awakening life with soft caress,
A world reborn, a sweet success.

The canvas stretches, vast and wide,
With every flower, dreams collide.
Each blossom tells a tale of grace,
In the heart's garden, our sacred space.

So let us cherish every sign,
In blossoms' glow, we intertwine.
With hope adorned across the sky,
Together we will always fly.

Enchanted Rays of Morning

Softly, the morning sun will rise,
Casting gold upon the skies.
A tapestry of light unfolds,
Each ray a story, brightly told.

In the hush of dawn's embrace,
Nature stirs, a secret place.
The world awakens, fresh and new,
In every heartbeat, life shines through.

With open eyes, we breathe it in,
A brand new day, let joy begin.
The light pours forth, a gentle stream,
Dancing with our waking dream.

In the whispers of the trees,
We find our hopes upon the breeze.
A promise held in morning's grace,
In every moment, a warm embrace.

Let us wander through this light,
Together in the morning bright.
For in each ray and soft caress,
We find the love that we possess.

The Dreamer's Canvas at Daybreak

The dawn paints colors soft and bright,
Whispers of dreams take gentle flight.
Brushstrokes of hope on morning's face,
Awakening hearts in a warm embrace.

With every hue, the past fades away,
New stories unfold, come what may.
The canvas stretches wide and free,
A masterpiece of possibility.

Sunrise spills over hills of gold,
Each ray a treasure waiting to unfold.
In every shadow, there's light to find,
A promise unspoken, whispers of the mind.

As day breaks forth, the dreams align,
Each heartbeat syncing with the divine.
The sky becomes a palette rare,
A sanctuary built from gentle care.

In the stillness, magic ignites,
Igniting the soul, dispelling the night.
The journey begins, step by step,
As dreamers awake, with every breath kept.

A Tapestry of Celestial Embrace

Stars weave tales across the night,
In silver threads, they catch the light.
Each constellation, a story old,
A tapestry in the heavens bold.

Galaxies spin on an endless wheel,
Whispers of the cosmos softly reveal.
Intertwined in a dance divine,
Hearts and hopes in the starlit line.

Dreams wrapped in celestial grace,
Floating freely in cosmic space.
The universe holds our silent screams,
In the tapestry woven from our dreams.

With every shooting star we chase,
We string our wishes in a sacred place.
Constellations blink with secrets free,
Painting destiny in shades of glee.

In this embrace, we find our way,
Through night's velvet, to the break of day.
Together we shine, like stars above,
A tapestry bound by endless love.

Flickers of Joy Amidst the Clouds

In the sky, the clouds drift slow,
Soft and tender, a gentle glow.
Flickers of joy peek through the gray,
A dance of light to brighten the day.

Sunbeams break like laughter's sound,
Chasing shadows that wrap around.
Each moment a sparkle, a glimpse of cheer,
Filling our hearts with warmth so near.

Raindrops fall but quickly fade,
Their fleeting touch, a cascade made.
Amidst the storm, there's beauty found,
In every drop, joy spins around.

As color bursts in nature's hold,
A tapestry bright, vivid and bold.
Flickers of memory, dancing free,
Remind us of all that it means to be.

In this fleeting world, we hold the light,
Casting away the endless night.
Embrace the joy that clouds unveil,
In their soft whispers, love will prevail.

Crescendos of Light in Quiet Moments

In quiet corners where shadows play,
Crescendos of light guide our way.
Each gentle pulse a heartbeat's song,
In serene beauty, we all belong.

The softest hues blend into one,
Illuminating paths where dreams run.
In stillness, our spirits take flight,
A ballet of whispers in fading light.

Moments unfold like petals in bloom,
Beneath the stars, dispelling the gloom.
Crescendos of grace in the silence found,
A symphony of peace in the heart's soft sound.

With every breath, we cherish the now,
Finding purpose in the sacred vow.
Light dances softly, a lover's embrace,
In the quiet, we discover our place.

Together we rise, united and free,
In crescendos of life, a shared decree.
Every moment cherished, every kiss of light,
In the beauty of quiet, our souls ignite.

Dappled Light Through Rain

The sun breaks through a curtain of gray,
Each droplet catches light at play.
Leaves glisten with the freshened glow,
A world reborn, in beauty's flow.

Soft whispers of the breeze unite,
In harmony with the soft twilight.
Colors dance on the pavement's sheen,
Reflecting dreams that might have been.

Nature's palette paints the scene,
A fleeting moment, calm and serene.
Winds carry scents of earth and rain,
A symphony that soothes the pain.

The earth exhales, and all is blessed,
In every droplet, in every crest.
With every step, a spark ignites,
In dappled light, the heart delights.

A love letter from the sky,
As rain and sun weave close and shy.
Moments captured, a fleeting sigh,
In dappled light, we learn to fly.

The Horizon's Gentle Call

Across the sea, where skies embrace,
A whisper rises, soft in space.
The horizon glows with warm delight,
An invitation into the night.

Waves lap gently, secrets shared,
Footprints linger, dreams repaired.
The edge of worlds is painted gold,
In that horizon, tales unfold.

Stars awaken as shadows blend,
The promise of a journey's end.
Horizons beckon, hearts abide,
In their vastness, love will guide.

Clouds drift slowly, stories woven,
In every color, essence stolen.
A dance of light, a canvas wide,
The horizon's call, our faithful guide.

Time stands still, under the spell,
Of whispers shared, we know it well.
For in that moment, spirits soar,
To where the horizon calls us more.

Among the Shards of Light

In shattered beams that flicker bright,
We weave our dreams with strands of light.
Each glimmer tells a story bold,
In vibrant hues, our hopes unfold.

Amidst the fragments, we find our way,
Guided by the stars that sway.
In twilight's grasp, we seek the dawn,
Among the shards, our souls are drawn.

Mirrors of the past twinkle near,
Reflecting whispers, joys, and fear.
Together we dance, in the glow,
Of every shard, our spirits grow.

The beauty lies in what we break,
In every piece, our hearts awake.
Among the shards, a treasure found,
In fragmented light, love is crowned.

So let the light guide our flight,
Through shadows shifting, day to night.
We stand united, hearts in flight,
Among the shards of endless light.

Kindling the Embered Skies

Under the glow of twilight's kiss,
We gather warmth in whispered bliss.
Fireside tales ignite the night,
As embered skies burn soft and bright.

With each flicker, memories stirred,
Hearts entwined, not a word heard.
In silence shared, our spirits dance,
Under the spell of fate's sweet chance.

Stars above like sparks of gold,
Glimmering promises, brave and bold.
A tapestry woven with love and care,
In the embered skies, we lay bare.

Through cracks of night, new dreams arise,
Bathed in the warmth of embered skies.
Each glow a wish, each flame a prayer,
In the stillness, we find our dare.

Let's kindle hope where shadows creep,
In every flicker, our dreams we keep.
Together we shine, no fear of falls,
As kindled hearts break down our walls.

Tender Luster in the Face of Time

In the quiet glow of dusk's embrace,
Memories whisper, soft as lace.
Fleeting shadows dance and play,
Holding moments, they fade away.

Gentle touches on weathered skin,
The warmth of love, where life begins.
Through the years, we learn to shine,
A tender luster, pure and divine.

Time may fade the brightest hue,
Yet in our hearts, it stays brand new.
In every wrinkle, tales reside,
Each mark a journey, lived with pride.

Seasons change, but we remain,
Holding tight through joy and pain.
Beneath the stars, we take our stance,
Embraced by fate's unyielding dance.

With every sunset's soft goodnight,
We find solace in fading light.
For in the twilight's gentle rhyme,
We hold the luster, face of time.

Serenity Rising on Luminous Winds

In the stillness of a breaking dawn,
Whispers of peace gracefully drawn.
Gentle breezes carry the sighs,
Of dreams awakened, in soft skies.

Golden rays touch the earth so light,
Transforming shadows into bright.
With every breath, serenity swells,
In the heart where tranquility dwells.

Clouds drift like thoughts, free and clear,
Echoes of hope for those who hear.
Luminous winds, they rise and glide,
Carrying love on the incoming tide.

Glowing embers of dawn's embrace,
Remind us all of time and space.
In the quietude, we find our way,
As serenity beckons us to stay.

With every moment that softly gleams,
We weave our lives into quiet dreams.
On luminous winds, let our spirits soar,
Finding solace on the cosmic shore.

Beneath the Brilliant Canopy Above

Stars twinkle bright in the velvet night,
Under the vast, enchanting sight.
Whispers of worlds far and wide,
Beneath the canopy, we confide.

Moonlight spills like silver grace,
Illuminating each hidden face.
In the hush, our secrets shared,
Bonded by dreams, deeply cared.

The night sings soft in gentle tones,
With every heartbeat, love atones.
Among the constellations' arc,
We find our way through the dark.

Clouds drift slowly, a soft embrace,
Holding our hopes in tranquil space.
Beneath this dome, we feel alive,
Where laughter and stillness thrive.

In the dark, our spirits rise,
Guided by starlit ties.
With every wish cast upon the sea,
Beneath the brilliant canopy, we're free.

Glimmers of Faith on the Horizon

In the distance, the sun starts to break,
Glimmers of hope across the lake.
Each ray dances, tender and true,
Whispers of faith, old yet anew.

The journey ahead, though steep and long,
Carries the echoes of a familiar song.
With every step, the spirit ignites,
A tapestry woven of daring flights.

Clouds may gather, dark and dense,
Yet in our hearts, we find the defense.
For in the trials and tempest's roar,
Glimmers of faith keep us wanting more.

Mountains rise, their peaks defined,
A pathway unfolds as we seek to find.
With courage brewing in our souls,
Hope dances vividly, making us whole.

As the horizon beckons its call,
We stand united, refusing to fall.
With every sunrise, our spirits ignite,
Glimmers of faith lead us to light.

Radiance in the Twilight

The sun dips low, a golden hue,
Casting shadows, night breaks through.
Stars twinkle softly, whispers in air,
In twilight's calm, all burdens wear.

The world holds still, as moments blend,
Where light and dark in silence mend.
A fleeting peace, a gentle sigh,
As dreams awaken, the night draws nigh.

Faint echoes linger of the day,
In colors soft, they fade away.
The horizon blushes, softly glows,
With secrets kept, the evening knows.

In this hush, our hearts unite,
A radiant glow, pure and bright.
Embrace the twilight's tender grace,
For in this calm, we find our place.

Together we stand, side by side,
In radiant twilight, we confide.
With every breath, let worries cease,
As love enfolds us in its peace.

Horizons Made of Dreams

Beyond the hills, where wishes soar,
Horizons beckon, tales of yore.
With every step, the path unfolds,
In shimmering light, our fate beholds.

A canvas vast, in colors bright,
Where shadows blend with morning light.
In the heart's embrace, we chase the dawn,
For dreams await on the dew-soaked lawn.

Dance with the clouds, rise high above,
Feel the warmth of a world that loves.
Each breath we take, a promise made,
A journey destined, never to fade.

Hold tight to visions, never let go,
As waves of dreams begin to flow.
In every heartbeat, find your song,
For in this world, we all belong.

With courage fierce, and spirits bold,
We paint our lives with hues of gold.
Horizons stretch, forever gleam,
In the night sky, we'll find our dream.

Shimmering Veil of Tomorrows

Mist and magic, a dawn's first light,
A shimmering veil, soft as the night.
Whispers of change dance through the air,
In this quiet pause, we find the rare.

Hope unfurls like petals in bloom,
Casting aside all shadows of gloom.
In the heart's whisper, futures arise,
As dreams take flight, beneath the skies.

Beyond the haze, a promise calls,
In the depths of night, our spirit sprawls.
Every heartbeat, a step ahead,
With love as our guide, no fear to tread.

The stars align, their stories weave,
In the tapestry of what we believe.
A shimmering cloak, our souls entwine,
As whispers of tomorrows brightly shine.

Together we'll journey, hand in hand,
Through valleys deep, on golden sand.
The veil of dreams, so rich, so bright,
In every moment, we chase the light.

Embracing the Luminous Dawn

As night surrenders to morning's grace,
We rise anew, to find our place.
With open hearts, we greet the day,
In the luminous dawn, we find our way.

Light spills softly on the horizon,
A canvas bright, where hope's begun.
In every ray, a promise shines,
With cherished dreams that intertwine.

Beneath the sky, a world awake,
With every step, new paths we make.
Embracing warmth, we let love flow,
As flowers bloom, and rivers glow.

With eyes alight, the future's near,
In every whisper, our dreams are clear.
Together we'll walk, side by side,
In the tender dawn, with hearts open wide.

Every challenge faced, we will withstand,
For in this light, we take our stand.
Embracing the dawn, both bold and true,
In love's embrace, we'll start anew.